TO THE READER

My prayer for you is that your relationship with God grows each day, with each prayer. My desire is you feel closer to Him, free in Him, and feel loved. I pray that through studying, praying, and believing, your life is forever changed. I believe that these things shall be so if you trust and believe in God.

21 Days of Prayer

Ebony Collins

Copyright © 2022 Ebony Collins

All rights reserved.

ISBN: 979-8-9851343-2-2

CONTENTS

	Acknowledgments	i
1	Positive Thinking	1
2	My Prayer Life	3
3	My Faith	5
4	My Giving	7
5	My Finances	9
6	My Career	11
7	My Lack	13
8	My Peace	15
9-12	Love Series	17
13	My Children	25
14	My Family	27
15	My Healing	29
16	My Anxiety	31
17	My Joy	33
18	My Fear	35
19	My Anger	37
20	Resisting Temptation	39
21	My Faithfulness to God	41

ACKNOWLEDGMENTS

They say that it takes 21 days to create habitual behavior. My prayer is that by joining me on this 21-day journey of praying, positive thinking, and intentional living, peace, and joy will become a habit. Take these 21 days with me and after you've completed day 21, go back to day 1.

DAY 1

TOPIC:
Positive Thinking

SCRIPTURE:
Philippians 4:8 Finally, brothers and sisters, whatever is true, whatever is noble, whatever is right, whatever is pure, whatever is lovely, whatever is admirable—if anything is excellent or praiseworthy—think about such things.

TRY THIS:
Today's affirmation is I control my day. Today will be a great day. Begin your day with a positive affirmation. Examples are: Today will be a productive day. I will be successful in my tasks today. I am capable of great achievements. I am worthy of wonderful things.

MESSAGE:
You can control the trajectory of your day by being positive and living in peace. Our minds are incredibly powerful. Have you ever been driving a car and noticed that when you start looking in a direction, left or right, the car starts to drift in that direction? It happens and that's because your mind is leaning, which causes you

to physically follow the same path. Our thoughts and actions are often connected. If I told you that your thoughts lead your actions, wouldn't that encourage you to think positively? Today's prayer is centered on our thoughts.

PRAYER:

Heavenly Father, I pray that you touch my mind and my thoughts. Help me to be positive as I travel through this day. I know that unexpected things are bound to happen and there will be hardships, but I pray that I will be reminded of your goodness. I pray that reference points of where you have shown yourself to me in the past, replace my moments of doubt. I trust you and believe you for all these things. In Jesus' name, I pray, Amen.

DAY 2

TOPIC:
My Prayer Life

SCRIPTURE:
1 Thessalonians 5:17-19 Pray without ceasing. In everything give thanks: for this is the will of God in Christ Jesus concerning you.

TRY THIS:
Today's affirmation is God hears me when I speak. Dedicate at least 5 minutes today to your relationship with God. Set an alarm for a time that you think will work best and pray in your own words. It can be a prayer of thanksgiving, a request, or just saying hello. Make this a priority.

MESSAGE:
Prayer is all about relationship. Each time we pray, we get closer to God. He hears us and He cares about us. To pray without ceasing is to always go to God in prayer. Regardless of what's going on in your life, you consult Him. You trust Him.

PRAYER:

Heavenly Father, I pray that you give me the words to say in prayer and when I don't have the words, accept my heart. Accept my confusion, sadness, and sometimes pain. Accept my anger and let my tears reach your ears. Accept what I have and replace it with what I need. In Jesus' name, Amen.

DAY 3

TOPIC:
My Faith

SCRIPTURE:
Matthew 17:20 He replied, "Because you have so little faith. Truly I tell you, if you have faith as small as a mustard seed, you can say to this mountain, 'Move from here to there,' and it will move. Nothing will be impossible for you."

TRY THIS:
Today's affirmation is I am believing God for all things, and He is supplying my needs. Remember a time when you were in need and didn't think you would make it. It could be a financial, emotional, or physical need. It could be health-related or career-related. Anything! Remember that time and then remember how you got through! Use this as your reference point of God's love for you.

MESSAGE:
Faith gets me by. I would easily give up when the going gets tough if it weren't for my faith that things will get better. Even if it's mustard seed faith, it's sufficient to make mountains move. Do you know how small a

mustard seed is and how large mountains are? Imagine what would happen as your faith grows.

PRAYER:

God, in moments of confusion, stress, and heartache, bring to my remembrance how you've helped me in the past and remind me that you have not changed. Help me to increase my faith in you. Remind me of how much you love me and how powerful you are. Accept my mustard seed for now and help me to increase that faith. I pray you continue to be present, mighty, and powerful in my life. In Jesus' name, Amen.

DAY 4

TOPIC:
My Giving

SCRIPTURE:
Luke 6:38 "Give, and it will be given to you. Good measure, pressed down, shaken together, running over, will be put into your lap. For with the measure you use it will be measured back to you."

TRY THIS:
Today's affirmation is I am generous and kind.
Give something to someone today. It could be $1 to someone on the street. You can give a compliment to someone.

MESSAGE:
Have you ever received a compliment or gift from someone? Have you ever been in a drive-through line and the person in front of you paid for your meal? How did you feel? For me, it changed my day. It made me smile. Make someone else feel that way today.

PRAYER:

Heavenly Father, help me to do something or say something that makes someone smile today. Help me to be kind, caring, considerate, and loving to your children. I know that there is joy in giving and I want to easily give that joy. In Jesus' name, Amen.

DAY 5

TOPIC:
My Finances

SCRIPTURE:
Proverbs 13:22 A good man leaves an inheritance to his children's children, but the sinner's wealth is laid up for the righteous.

TRY THIS:
Today's affirmation is I am wise and wealthy. Take 5% of what's in your account and store it away for 90 days praying for God to multiply it. You can place it in a savings account, in your bible, or just somewhere safe where you will remember. If you're like me you may need to set a reminder in your phone with the amount, location, and when the 90 days have expired.

MESSAGE:
You could have all the money in the world but if you don't know what to do with it, you can lose it in a day. We frequently pray for what we want but we forget to pray for the wisdom to know what to do with it. How to grow it. How to invest, spend, save. Having

everything means nothing without knowledge.

PRAYER:

Heavenly Father, I pray you give me the wisdom and abilities to be financially intelligent. Help me to save for the future, to not spend frivolously, and to be giving with what you have blessed me with. Help me to make good financial choices that will lead to my wealth, independence, and continued success. In Jesus' name, Amen.

DAY 6

TOPIC:
My Career

SCRIPTURE:
2 Thessalonian 3:10 For even when we were with you, we gave you this rule: "The one who is unwilling to work shall not eat."

TRY THIS:
Today's affirmation is I am destined for greatness. Think about one career goal that you have for yourself. Write down the goal and two things that you can do before the end of this quarter to move toward that goal.

MESSAGE:
If we don't work, we don't eat. That was true in Bible days and it's true today. The problem is that we are tired of working and being unfulfilled. No one wants to work for a paycheck. You deserve to love what you do. You deserve to do what you love. Sometimes we have to do what we don't want to do until we can move into our destiny. Never give up! Never settle. Do what you have to do to get where you deserve to be.

PRAYER:

Heavenly Father, I pray you take control of my future and my goals. Show me the path I should travel and the choices I should make. Let me walk in your light and my purpose. I don't want to work just for money, but I want to work for your glory. God guide me into what will give me satisfaction, peace, and fulfillment. Guide me into what gives me joy. Let my work but acceptable unto you. In Jesus' name, Amen.

DAY 7

TOPIC:
My Lack

SCRIPTURE:
Philippians 4:19 And my God will meet all your needs according to the riches of his glory in Christ Jesus.

TRY THIS:
Today's affirmation is: All my needs shall be met. I lack nothing. Listen to God Provides by Tamela Mann.

MESSAGE:
We look at our circumstances and we see what we need. We see what we desire, and we see the gaps. Stop looking at what is missing and take more time to acknowledge what you have. God will provide for every need in His time. It's challenging when His timing doesn't match ours, but His is perfect! Trust Him.

PRAYER:

God, whatever I lack, I trust you to provide. I trust you to give me what I need and not only what I want. If my desires don't line up with your will in my life, I pray you block it and give me understanding. I thank you for keeping me even in the moments when I feel alone. I pray you use those moments to send the Holy Spirit to comfort me and remind me of your purpose for me and your plan to take care of me. In Jesus' name, Amen.

DAY 8

TOPIC:
My Peace

SCRIPTURE:
Philippians 4:7 And the peace of God, which transcends all understanding, will guard your hearts and your minds in Christ Jesus.

TRY THIS:
Today's affirmation is I am at peace in all things. Take 10 minutes to sit in silence. Don't use social media or talk on the phone. However, listening to music is a reasonable option. Sit and just be. Be you. Don't think about bills, responsibilities, or anything that has the possibility of causing stress. Even if you steal this moment in the car before entering home or work. You need time to just be before you have to be anything to anyone else.

MESSAGE:
Sometimes peace is silence. Sometimes peace is reading a book. You may find peace in sitting in your car or taking a shower. I enjoy listening to my music in the car alone when I'm in my driveway. Peace is what you

make it, so you have to make it a necessity.

PRAYER:

God, I pray for a peace that surpasses all understanding. Fill me up with it so that no matter what comes my way, it will be met with peace. Regardless of the circumstances, trials, heartache, or confusion, I need inner peace. Not peace that is controlled by circumstance, but the peace that is deep within. The peace that the world didn't give so the world cannot take it away. Calm my spirit, God. In Jesus' name, Amen.

DAY 9

TOPIC:
Loving Myself

SCRIPTURE:
Psalm 139:14 I praise you because I am fearfully and wonderfully made; your works are wonderful, I know that full well.

TRY THIS:
Today's affirmation is God made me the way I am on purpose. Listen to In Spite of Me by Tasha Cobbs Leonard.

MESSAGE:
God is perfect. He makes no mistakes. When He looks at you, He sees a masterpiece. Every flaw that you point out about yourself, is beauty in His eyes. He handcrafted you, the way He needs you to be. Your eyes, hair, lips, any blemishes you find, were all His doing. Know that He loves you so much and you deserve the love. You deserve God's love, and you deserve your love. Love on yourself because you are worthy. Let no person make you question your worth.

PRAYER:

God, I want to love me as you love me. I want to look in the mirror and see God's perfection and not the flaws. Help me to see me the way you see me. Help me to put on my heavenly glasses and adore myself because I was created in your image. Help me to demand the love that I deserve from the world and to walk away from situations that leave me feeling void and unworthy. In Jesus' name, Amen.

DAY 10

TOPIC:
Loving Others

SCRIPTURE:
1 Peter 4:8 Above all, love each other deeply, because love covers over a multitude of sins.

TRY THIS:
Today's affirmation is I love others as God loves me. Tell someone you love them today.

MESSAGE:
God loves us in a way that a parent loves their child. Until you have a child, you cannot understand the heart of it, but as someone's child, you can relate to how that love feels. God gives it to us without us deserving it, and we should aim to be more like Him. Give others the same love we receive without asking.

PRAYER:

Heavenly Father, I pray you help me to love like you. When people encounter me, I pray that feel the genuineness of my heart and it warms them. I pray I will be able to change someone's spirit and positively alter their day with the love in my heart. In Jesus' name, Amen.

DAY 11

TOPIC:
Romantic Love

SCRIPTURE:
1 Corinthians 13:4-8 Love is patient, love is kind. It does not envy, it does not boast, it is not proud. It does not dishonor others, it is not self-seeking, it is not easily angered, it keeps no record of wrongs. Love does not delight in evil but rejoices with the truth. It always protects, always trusts, always hopes, always perseveres. Love never fails. But where there are prophecies, they will cease; where there are tongues, they will be stilled; where there is knowledge, it will pass away.

TRY THIS:
Today's affirmation is I deserve good love. Think about the type of person you want to spend your life with. If you are currently with that person, send them a loving text. If you have not found that person, consider if you are open to love. Is your heart open? Is your mind open? Are you ready for love?

MESSAGE:

Love is beautiful, precious, unique, and long-lasting. The biblical definition of love encompasses all. Understand that you need to give that type of love and you deserve to receive that type of love from a partner. If you

PRAYER:

Heavenly Father, I pray you create a love in my life that resembles your love for me. Create a love for me that doesn't disrupt my peace or interrupt my blessings in any way. Give me a love that enhances my life. Give me a partner that is capable of receiving my love and worthy of my genuine heart. Prepare me for the love that you planned for me. Prepare my heart and heal any brokenness that's within that would prevent me from being ready for love. In Jesus name, Amen.

DAY 12

TOPIC:
Significant Other

SCRIPTURE:
Genesis 2:18 The LORD God said, "It is not good for the man to be alone. I will make a helper suitable for him."

TRY THIS:
Today's affirmation is: (Insert partners name) will be covered by God's grace and mercy.
Write a love note to your partner. This could be via text or email but handwritten would be classic. Make sure they receive it before the end of the day.

MESSAGE:
To love and be loved is a beautiful thing. It's a blessing. So many people are searching or waiting to find the person God made for them. When you have that person in your life, you want to nurture that relationship. Protect the relationship and watch it grow.

PRAYER:

Heavenly Father, I pray you shield (insert name) and cover them in your protection. Dispatch your angels to surround them and carry them through their rough days. Let them feel your love and my love even now. Keep them encouraged, confident in you, and at peace in their heart. Thank you for placing them in my life and I pray that they have joy and success. In Jesus' name, Amen.

DAY 13

TOPIC:
My Children

SCRIPTURE:
Psalm 127:3 Children are a heritage from the LORD, offspring a reward from him.

TRY THIS:
Today's affirmation is: The children that I love are protected and blessed. Have a conversation with one of the children in your life. Listen to them and reassure them that you love them, and you care about what they have to say.

MESSAGE:
Whether you are a parent, aunt/uncle, friend, teacher, or neighbor, we all have children that we care about. In caring for those children, we become invested in their safety, joy, and their futures. We must remind the children that we hear them, and we care about them. Naturally, we must teach and guide them but don't forget to also cover them in prayer.

PRAYER:

Father God, I pray that you protect the children who are in my heart. Cover them with your grace and your mercy. Dispatch your angels to surround them and fight their battles. Equip them with heavenly armor in their minds so they may fight the temptations of the enemy. Lead them down a path of righteousness. Remind them in moments of despair that you are their help. Remind them in moments of weakness that you are their strength. Let them be carefree, enjoying the joys of childhood. I pray your love penetrates their heart and they forever feel that love. In Jesus' name, Amen.

DAY 14

TOPIC:
My Family

SCRIPTURE:
Psalm 133:1 How good and pleasant it is when God's people live together in unity!

TRY THIS:
Today's affirmation is: My family is strong, protected, and blessed. Reach out to someone in your family that you don't talk to daily. Tell them that you love them. This can be done via text, social media, or email. If you want, you can call.

MESSAGE:
Family is important. Some have a plethora of blood relatives who add immense value to their lives. Others have a select few but those relationships are valuable. Easily, we allow life to take over and responsibilities to alienate us from what matters. Family matters and you have to be available for what matters.

PRAYER:

God, please cover and protect my family. Let them feel my love and your love as they travel through their lives. Help me to be what they need and lift them. Please let the ones who are in my life regularly be good for me, adding value, and let the distant ones be blessed. Protect them all from the plans of the enemy and let them live in the promises of you. Heal any family hurt and mend any separation. In Jesus' name, Amen.

DAY 15

TOPIC:
Healing

SCRIPTURE:
Jeremiah 17:14 Heal me, LORD, and Will be healed; save me and I will be saved, for you are the one I praise.

TRY THIS:
Today's affirmation is I am healed and whole.
Listen to I'm Still Here by Dorinda Clark-Cole.

MESSAGE:
When we are afflicted physically or mentally, it takes a toll on us. We can begin to question God, but I want you to know that nothing is allowed to happen without God's permission. Remembering that He created us, I ask you, why would He create someone just to destroy them? He wouldn't. Every ailment, every pain, every hurt has a purpose. Find the purpose and praise Him in the midst.

PRAYER:

Heavenly Father, most merciful God I come to thank you today. I thank you for the hurt, I thank you for the aches, I thank you for the pain. I thank you for what I have to go through because I know greater is what I'm getting to. I pray that you continue to help me through this. I trust you for total healing and revelation. I trust that the lesson in this will be one that will help me to help another. I speak healing over my life. I speak wholeness over my mind and my body and trust you fully to deliver that which I claim in your name. In Jesus' name, Amen.

DAY 16

TOPIC:
Anxiety

SCRIPTURE:
1 Peter 5:7 Cast all your anxiety on him because he cares for you.

TRY THIS:
Today's affirmation is I can't control the future, but my future is controlled. Everything is going to be alright. Listen to God Provides by Tamela Mann. Sometimes we don't know what's next and we get anxious, but I need you to remember that God will provide everything in your life. He has it mapped out even when you feel lost.

MESSAGE:
We can feel the overwhelming need to know what's next. I encourage you to learn how to release the control and solely depend on God. Trust that He has your best interest at heart. Jeremiah 29:11 says that God has a plan to prosper us and not to harm us. That tells us that what's unpredictable to us, was planned out for Him.

PRAYER:

Heavenly Father, calm the anxiousness inside of me. Remind me that I have a purpose and you have a plan. Help me to see you in all things even when it looks bleak. I want to walk in the peace of knowing you have my back, and you have me covered. In Jesus' name, Amen.

DAY 17

TOPIC:
My Joy

SCRIPTURE:
2 Thessalonian 3:10 For even when we were with you, we gave you this rule: "The one who is unwilling to work shall not eat."

TRY THIS:
Today's affirmation is I am joyful. Smile today. Smile right now. Think of something funny and laugh. Watch something funny.

MESSAGE:
I love the way Kirk Franklin said that happiness is based on something happening, but joy can't be taken. That is because joy comes from God and lives within you. The world can't take what the world didn't give you.

PRAYER:

Heavenly Father, I thank you for the joy you have given me. I thank you for the ability to smile and laugh amid challenging times. I thank you for the laughter that fills my belly when I least expect it. I thank you for the people you placed in my life that bring light about them and comedy to the room. I thank you for the moments I feel the joy in my heart. Let me never forget who my joy comes from and that it lives as long as you live in my heart. In Jesus' name, Amen.

DAY 18

TOPIC:
My Fear

SCRIPTURE:

Isaiah 41:13 For I am the LORD your God who takes hold of your right hand and says to you, do not fear; I will help you.

TRY THIS:

Today's affirmation is I am bold and fearless. Listen to God Blocked it by Kurt Carr. Fear is a normal emotion, but God will block the things set out to destroy you. He will protect you.

MESSAGE:

Life is scary and the consequences of our decisions are real. We cannot live in fear because that will hold us back from everything that God has for us. Risks produce rewards. So, while you cannot live in fear, you can live with fear. You must do it while afraid. Fear can restrain you or propel you. You choose.

PRAYER:

God, I pray that you remove the fear that grows inside of me. Give me peace and give me comfort in knowing that you would never leave me nor forsake me. Help me to replace my fear with faith because fear makes me retreat and my faith will lead me to rejoice! In Jesus' name, Amen.

DAY 19

TOPIC:
My Anger

SCRIPTURE:
Proverbs 15:1 A gentle answer turns away wrath, but a harsh word stirs up anger.

TRY THIS:
Today's affirmation is I will think before I speak and maintain my composure. When responding to people today, I want you to take a deep breath before you speak. After a deep breath, I want you to think about what you are going to say. This is maybe a 5-second delay in conversation but it's worth it.

MESSAGE:
People are trying. When I say that I say it with experience. People can push all your buttons, even the ones you never knew existed, but your reaction will speak more about you than them. You have to be slow to respond, think about the consequences of your words and actions, and then make a conscious

choice about what you say and do. What do you want your response to say about you? It's not about what the other person deserves, it's about who you are. We all get angry, and this isn't to discourage that natural emotion. My goal is to encourage you in your handling of that anger.

PRAYER:

God, I pray that you help me to control my responses to negative situations. Help me to be slow to anger, considerate of people who aren't considerate of me, and calm in moments that would have filled me with rage. The enemy will try to disrupt my peace and fill me with rage, but God, you live within me, and I want your spirit to come out of me. In Jesus' name, Amen.

DAY 20

TOPIC:
Resisting Temptation

SCRIPTURE:
1 Corinthian 10:13 No temptation[a] has overtaken you except what is common to mankind. And God is faithful; he will not let you be tempted[b] beyond what you can bear. But when you are tempted,[c] he will also provide a way out so that you can endure it.

TRY THIS:
Today's affirmation is I am stronger than my weaknesses. Deny yourself of something today. For me, it would be fast food because it's my weakness. For you, it could be candy, social media, a specific person. It could be anything that you overindulge in.

MESSAGE:
Temptation comes in various forms and the enemy can be a tricky little thing. He will use the things and people you love to try and turn you to his side, but you must be wiser. The temptation will start small and then spiral

out of control. If your weakness is food, it may start with a sale on unhealthy snacks or a loved one offering you a snack that you were staying away from. The enemy will use the people you least expect, and they won't know they are being used. You'll accept the small snack and BAM; you've opened the door for fast food and everything you had been trying to resist. If we can deny ourselves of the things, we love but know are no good for us, we're more likely to resist temptation from the enemy. You have to be strong and walk away from some people, places, and things.

PRAYER:

God, I pray that you give me the strength to say no when a yes isn't pleasing to you. I pray that you give me the strength to go left when desire is pulling me to the right. Give me the courage to abstain from the things that would make me a bad representative of you and all that you represent. Help me to resist that which is unlike you. In Jesus' name, Amen.

DAY 21

TOPIC:
My Faithfulness to You

SCRIPTURE:

Matthew 22:37 Jesus replied: "'Love the Lord your God with all your heart and with all your soul and with all your mind.'[a]

TRY THIS:

Today's affirmation is I will choose God every time. Listen to Blue God by Jessica Reedy. Imagine the way we hurt God when He does so much for us and reward Him by choosing Him when it's convenient.

MESSAGE:

We want God to be faithful to us, but we fail at being faithful to Him. Don't treat Him like an option, He's the only choice. If you keep giving Him your burdens after you've tried to fix them, you're just wasting time. Let God do what He does best. Hand over your burdens AND your praise. Don't just call Him when you are in distress, call Him to thank Him just because.

PRAYER:

God, I'm sorry if I ever treated you like an option. I say yes to you today. Yes, I choose you. Yes, I will go where you tell me to go. Yes, I will do what you tell me to do. I will love who you tell me to love. Even when it's hard and I feel they don't deserve it, I will forgive who you tell me to forgive. I give you a yes today! In Jesus' name, Amen.

BONUS PRAYER

TOPIC:
Forgiveness

SCRIPTURE:
Ephesians 4:32 Be kind and compassionate to one another, forgiving each other, just as in Christ God forgave you.

TRY THIS:
Today's affirmation is I won't allow hurt from the past to hurt me today. Write down something that you are holding onto. Write down exactly what happened and how it made you feel. After you've written it down, rip the paper up. Release your hurt and extend forgiveness with each tear to the paper.

MESSAGE:
We serve a loving and forgiving God. We are blessed for that reason. We need His forgiveness because we mess up so much. We make mistakes, we sin, and we turn our backs on Him repeatedly. How does He repay us? With forgiveness and unconditional love. He still sees the amazing creation that He blessed the world with. For that reason alone, we ought to forgive others. We do nothing to deserve the forgiveness, we just

receive it. Furthermore, harboring hurt takes away the space for God's blessings. Let go of the pain. Release the betrayal. Free yourself of the hurt.

PRAYER:

Heavenly Father, I pray that you help me to heal from hurt inflicted on me by others. Help me to forgive those who have done me wrong. Help me to forgive those who have lied to me and lied on me. Help me to forgive those who have betrayed me and deliberately hurt me. Help me to heal from the anger, stress, and frustration. Instill in me a greater desire to be more like you and to be closer to you. I want to forgive like you and love like you. Let me harbor no anger or malice in my heart toward others. Let me have peace in all situations. In Jesus' name, Amen.

ABOUT THE AUTHOR

Ebony Collins is an award-winning author, Licensed Life Coach Minister, mother, and wife. Her mission is to encourage God's people and show them, genuine love, while inspiring them to pursue their goals.

Made in the USA
Middletown, DE
05 September 2023